RISE UP,
AIM HIGH,
STAND TALL &
BE OUTSTANDING
in the field of business & life

c. michelle bryant-griffin

DEDICATION

To my husband Benny.
Thanks for your unconditional understanding, love and support. Without
you there would be no Focus on Fabulous,
no dream ignited, no little yellow "be" book.

And to all the hard-working people trying to not only make
a living but keep your sanity, find yourself and
leave a legacy worthy of heart and efforts.

FORWARD

When I was asked to review the new book on ideas for entrepreneurs by my friend and colleague Michelle Bryant-Griffin, I was delighted. I know Michelle to be creative and insightful and full of ideas. I know her to be a champion of entrepreneurs and to always be on the look-out for opportunities and silver linings.

This book is completely Michelle.

Her wisdom is deep, her observations are keen, her heart is evident on every page. She cares deeply about the success of everyone she touches. She cares deeply about You.

Michelle digs a little deeper into what attributes are required in a successful entrepreneur. She focuses on who you must become to be successful in business. Success in not just a result of your knowledge or your actions. Success comes from inside. It comes from how you treat others, how you motivate yourself, and how your share yourself with the world.

This book is a great combination of common sense, shared experience, and challenges to the status quo that will have you looking at yourself in a different way. Reading this book and applying its lessons will change you. It will remind you, encourage you, and invite you to become the best you can be.
This is indeed a book that needs to be on the bookshelf of every entrepreneur.

Kartyna Johnson, J.D.
~ Owner Mirelli Entrepreneur Training for Women

Chapter 1. **Be** your customer

Chapter 2. **Be** honest

Chapter 3. **Be** different

Chapter 4. **Be** a backer

Chapter 5. **Be** transparent & vulnerable

Chapter 6. **Be** positive

Chapter 7. **Be** patient & accepting

Chapter 8. **Be** brave

Chapter 9. **Be** willing to fail

Chapter 10. **Be** a beacon

This little book is designed to compile several topics from various sources, experiences and experts to offer a comprehensive outlet toward running a successful business and live a fulfilling life. May you glean some nuggets from its contents and prosper as a result.

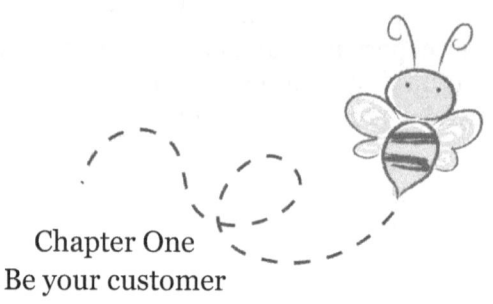

Chapter One
Be your customer

Get closer than ever to your customers. So close, in fact, that you tell them what they need well before they realize it themselves. (Steve Jobs)

Not too long ago I did a video entitled Are You Open for Business? It came out of my frustration in trying to reach a local small business that I had a potential client to give her. After the first phone call informed me her mailbox was full, I waited another business day and tried again only to get the same message. At which point I emailed her and sent a private Facebook message. A week went by and no reply. As a small business owner, I could not imagine not being accessible for an entire week to potential customers.
It doesn't matter how good your product or service is if no one can reach you. Look at your business through your customer's eyes and be available.

It is it important to answer the phone and reply to emails because you are responsible for letting people know about your product and how it will benefit them. People will not buy anything form you if they don't want it or if feel they don't need it. As well you will not be able to persuade them that they want or need to purchase what you're offering unless you understand exactly what your customers desire. You must also make sure that you understand what benefits your product or service offers to your customers. Often, we get so busy in the "business" aspects of running our businesses that we lose sight of the needs of our customer or who our ideal client may be.

At one point early in my entrepreneur journey, I was confident I knew without a doubt who my ideal customer was, only to discover I was completely off base. With the help of my business mentor, by tackling stats and tracking data, I was able to pinpoint my exact customer and target audience. Knowing and understanding your customer and their needs is at the center of every successful business, whether that business sells directly to individuals or other businesses.

As you identify your customer, you may also recognize the need for value, not just in the product or service but also in the relationship. You will quickly appreciate that your customers are your greatest asset and gain the value they bring to your business in ways other than monetarily.

Ask yourself: What do you know about your present and potential customers? The more you know about them, the more effective your efforts will be in marketing and closing the sale.

Ask yourself:
• who they are (characteristics like age, gender, education level, where they live, their hobbies, etc.)
• what they buy
• why they buy it

If your business sells products or services to other businesses is then you'll need to know who is responsible for the actual purchasing decision. You can also learn a lot about your customers by just talking to them. Ask them why they're buying or not buying for that matter. Ask them what they may want to purchase later. Ask about other needs they may have. This can give you a valued picture of what's important to them now and in the future. Try sending them a simple five-question survey. Sites like Survey Monkey offer them for free.

Solid sales are driven by focusing on the benefits that your product or service can bring to your customers. If you know what obstacles face them, it is easier to offer creative solutions. It is imperative that you know what you bring to the table before your actual encounter.

Knowing and keeping up with the trends will influence your customers. Therefore, this helps you get ahead of what your customers need and allows you to offer it to them as soon as they need it.

HERE ARE SOME THINGS YOU SHOULD KNOW ABOUT YOUR CUSTOMER:

1. Know who they are
If your company sells directly to individuals, it behooves you to find out your customers' gender, age, marital status, occupation, etc. If you sell to other businesses, you should find out what size and type of business they are. The more you know about your client's the better and more precise products or services you can provide to fit what they need.

2. Know what they do
If your business sells directly to individuals, you should know their occupations and interests. If you sell to other businesses, this information helps you understand what their business is trying to achieve. This is especially effective if you both have a common goal or vision.

3. Know why they prefer to purchase
Knowing why customers buy a product or service make it easier to match their needs to the specific benefits offered by your business.

4. Know when they purchase
If you approach a customer only when they want to buy, you will increase your chances of success immensely. As such, if you catch them at the wrong time you could potentially lose the sale altogether.

5. Know how they purchase
Many people prefer to purchase online, while others prefer to meet one on one or face-to face. It is imperative to know which method your customer prefers.

6. Know how much money they can spend
If you know what your customers budget is, you'll be more successful if you are able to match what you're offering with what your customer can afford. You don't want to undersell yourself but don't start your price point at a place you know is out of their reach either.

7. Know what makes them feel good about their purchase
If you know what makes your customers happy then you can serve them in ways they prefer. For example, if you know they value a good deal, or quality, or prefer buying in bulk, you will be more likely to close the sale. It is important to find out what makes them proud of their purchase decision.

8. Know what they expect of your company
For example, if your customers expect a quality product at a reasonable price and you don't disappoint them, you stand to gain repeat business. I prefer to adopt an attitude of "under promise and over deliver."

9. Know what they think about you
If your customers enjoy their business relationship with you, they're likely to buy more and refer others. As well, you can only tackle problems that customers have if you know what they are.

10. Know what they think about your competitors
If you know how your customers feel about your competition, you can get the upper hand and stand a better chance of staying ahead of your rivals.

Ultimately, your goal is to create a healthy, profitable, long-term relationship with customers that provide value to both parties. The only way this will work is to provide a relationship that is win-win. That only happens when you take the time to put yourself in the shoes of your customer. By doing so you'll be more successful if you can be your customer.

RECAP: Contacts or customers take time to build. Nourish the soil to produce great growth and blooming relationships

Chapter 2
Be honest

Honesty is the best policy.
(Benjamin Franklin)

This probably should have been chapter one because having honesty and integrity in the workplace is probably one of the most important qualities of great leadership in business. Let's start off with this great quote by Jon Huntsman, Sr., a multibillionaire who started a chemical company from scratch and grew it into a $12 billion enterprise from his book, <u>Winners Never Cheat</u>. He writes, *"There are no moral shortcuts in the game of business or life. There are, basically, three kinds of people, the unsuccessful, the temporarily successful, and those who become and remain successful. The difference is character."*

Running a business that takes pride in being ethical and forthright is a challenge, and many companies end up compromising in various ways in the name of profit. More than likely, if you were to dig deep into those companies, you'd find honesty isn't viewed as an important characteristic. Ironically, it's nearly impossible for a business to build trust if honesty isn't a strong belief in how that company handles aspects of its work process. Many entrepreneurs start their own companies, in part, because they long to work in an atmosphere that matches their values. They are searching for honest businesses.

Honesty and integrity go hand in hand. But unfortunately, the notions of business and honesty don't always go hand in hand. But great leaders possess both integrity and honesty. Leaders with integrity aren't afraid of the truth. Integrity means telling the truth even if the truth isn't pretty. Leaders keep their promises. They make them carefully, even reluctantly, but once they have given that promise, they follow that promise through without fail.

In business, there should be no exceptions to honesty and integrity. Integrity is a state of mind and is not based on situations or circumstances. As such, if you compromise your integrity in small situations despite the size or merit of the consequence, it then becomes easy to compromise on the big ones.

Successful business leaders with integrity always err on the side of fairness. In fact, the true mark of leadership is how fair you can be when other people treat you unfairly.

When you create a workplace environment or culture built on honesty, you also help foster workplace behavior and activity that is consistent despite external influences. Many successful companies spend years building a foundation of loyalty and trust. The best way for building that trust is honesty. When customers perceive that a business does things the right way and cares about creating a quality product or service, they tend to reward that business. The values and trust the business has built with customers, and employees serve to hold strong reputations. People are looking for companies that not only sell products and services, but also in some way make the world better, brighter, or a more meaningful place.

It takes three kinds of honesty to achieve this honest approach to business.

<u>Honesty with others.</u> Sounds simple enough, but it goes beyond not lying to your customers and employees.

It's more about owning a mistake when you mess up and admitting when you're wrong. It's also about not pretending to be something you're not. It requires recognizing the state of the business to yourself, and your employees. And, when it comes to customers, it requires selling only what you can deliver effectively and most importantly, always living up to your word.

When done correctly, this kind of honesty gets a tremendous amount of loyalty from customers as well as employees. They both know they can trust you and more importantly, that you value the integrity of the relationship.

<u>Honesty with self.</u> You are often your own worst critic, but it is imperative that you be brutally honest with yourself about what you really want—from your job, your experience, and your business. For a business to work well, the leader needs to be fulfilled. Too often, however, you end up running businesses that don't give you what you want. Often, it's small dishonesties along the way that causes you to make compromises with your business that lead to this dissatisfaction. You tell yourself you need to do tasks you don't like, and end up creating jobs you don't enjoy, or let other's definitions of success trample your own. You eventually build companies that aren't in sync with your vision.

<u>Honesty about the experience.</u> Often as business owners, you strive so hard for perfection and gloss over imperfections. That's understandable—you're in the business of attracting clients and instilling consumer confidence. But what your customers and clients don't realize is that, while you don't need to publicly sound the alarm each time you have a concern, there's a cost that comes with claiming that everything is all roses. It not only makes you unrelatable to your peers, but it also skews your own perspective about the business.

When you embarked on your journey to start your business, you wanted to know about the real-life challenges and tough decisions that other entrepreneurs faced. You wondered if you would find people who were willing to drop the "perfection act" and share some of their "mishaps and mistakes." Surprisingly they were being easier to find than you thought, and they were willing to share when they had been right and when they had been wrong. But more importantly, they were willing to share what they still didn't know. They didn't try to portray their business in a certain light. Being honest about their experience gave them clarity and direction and their honesty made them seem more competent and confident.

But please realize, just being honest won't keep you in business. It will keep you happy with your business. And that's the true definition of success. After all, do what you love, and you'll never work a day in your life.

RECAP: If it's not right - don't do it. If it's not true – don't say it. Simple.

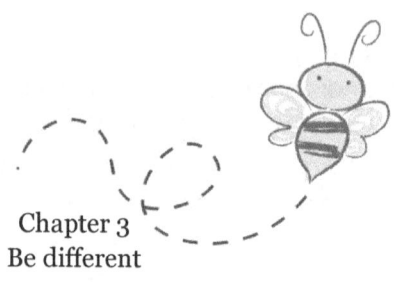

Chapter 3
Be different

Fitting in allows you to blend in with everyone else. But being different allows you to be yourself, to be unique and be more creative.
(Sonya Parker)

To have a competitive edge in business you must think differently and be a bit bolder than the competition. In lay terms, you've got to think outside of the box. There is a quote that states, *"The one who follows the crowd will usually go no further than the crowd. Those who walk alone are likely to find themselves in places no one has ever been before."* This powerful message is important yet is often overlooked by people not heeding its warning. No matter what it pertains to, from love and life, to business and marketing, copying what your competitors are doing and failing to forge your own path can be an extremely unfavorable mistake.

Now three-year old's have iPads, and middle schoolers are getting smartphones. Do we truly need or want these things? Yes, but not just because they are trendy but because everyone else has them. We don't want to be the last one. We don't usually like to be different or to stand out.

Thankfully, we grow up and realize the delusion to trying to be normal. We start to become individuals who value who we are and what we've become.

We learn to appreciate that being different can be beautiful. But while we begin to celebrate being different on a personal level, it does not always translate into our professional lives.

We learn to appreciate that being different can be beautiful. But while we begin to celebrate being different on a personal level, it does not always translate into our professional lives.

I think Steve Jobs said it best in his "Think Different" campaign with this quote: *"Here's to the crazy ones. The misfits. The rebels. The trouble-makers. The round pegs in the square holes. The ones who see things differently. They're not fond of rules, and they have no respect for the status-quo. You can quote them, disagree with them, glorify, or vilify them. But the only thing you can't do is ignore them. Because they change things. They push the human race forward. And while some may see them as the crazy ones, we see genius. Because the people who are crazy enough to think they can change the world, are the ones who do."* When creating the iMac, one of Steve's designers happened to color his rendition. When asked why, he responded, "It's different. computers are usually a boring beige color." That's where the Think Different campaign was birthed. Simply by someone stepping out, taking a chance, and thinking outside the box.

You have something the world needs and playing small does no good to anyone. Even if you are in an MLM industry you have a unique gift or quality that sets you apart from others selling your exact product or service. Find it. Use it. Capitalize on it.
There is power in being different. You're an entrepreneur, rejoice in the fact that you set the rules. In most companies, being different isn't even tracked let alone appreciated. There are some brilliant people out there. Some are superstars.

The key to being different in your business is to do it in a way that is highly relevant to your audience.

Be different in a way that creates a competitive advantage. And that is not easy.

Here are some tips on how businesses can go about being different:

1) <u>Challenge conventional business models</u>:
When starting a new venture do not assume the conventional business model is the right one for you and your business – challenge the status quo to find what is right for you and your vision.

2) <u>Work together to get new talent:</u>
Seeking young, fresh talent will help develop a new generation of pioneers, whose creativity may otherwise be hindered at a larger organization.

3) <u>Keep your friends close:</u>
A positive brand reputation originated from those customers and fans who are early supporters of your product will raise awareness and maximize sales needed to be engaging with as many audiences and consumer groups as possible.

4) <u>Don't forget the product:</u>
That's where business starts, with a product, idea or service. As ventures develop, business leaders often get so distracted with keeping up with the growth and building a brand that they forget the product at the core. You can have a great business model, but if your product isn't up to standards, your business is unlikely to flourish. Keep your product or service at the heart of everything you do, making sure that it is the best it can be.

5) <u>Think boldly:</u>
Don't be dissuaded – and don't believe that making noise simply for the sake of it will provide you with a free industry admission ticket. To be viewed as different, consider going back to square one and challenging an absolute industry basic, the heart of the status quo.

RECAP: You can't stand out when you look like everyone else unless you are the tallest, biggest most radiant flower in the field.

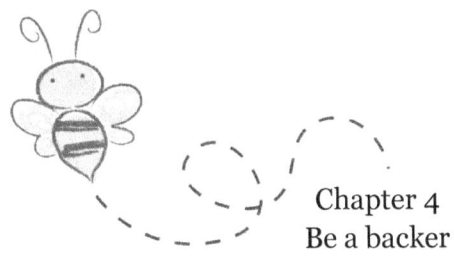

Chapter 4
Be a backer

As you navigate through the rest of your life, be open to collaboration. Other people and their ideas are often better than your own. Find a group of people who challenge and inspire you, spend a lot of time with them, and it will change your life.
(Amy Poehler)

Being an entrepreneur takes a special person, attitude, and mindset. Not everyone is wired to be an entrepreneur and as such, we are often a misunderstood breed. I think I've always known I had that in my blood but didn't really accept it until later in life. Now there is no turning back. One major key to becoming a successful small business owner is collaboration.

I am known as a connector in my business circles. I am continually setting up one business owner with another owner or opportunity. I regularly give social media shout outs about my colleagues and area small businesses. I collaborate with local and long-distance small business owners to bring success and growth to both our businesses through partnering. I have an advisory board and have been involved with several local and national organization such as SCORE and ABWA and have a local "tribe" that I rely on weekly for accountability, business guidance, and assessment and ideas when my well runs dry.

Having a person or persons to back you in all areas of your business is vital. I think it takes several people. Perhaps one that backs you when you want to quit. One that backs your creative juices, one for promotional ideas and so forth. As well, you should back other businesses. Be involved in what they are doing. Share in their successes and be proud of their accomplishments.

As a small business owner, it can often feel hard to compete with the large corporations. But by joining forces with other small businesses you can harness the power of the community and grow together. Seek out collaborative relationships, formally or informally, with other like-minded businesses and individuals and stop thinking of them as competitors.

Not too long after I started my business, I discovered a locally owned restaurant where I live and met the owner at one of her events held there. She told her story of buying the place, purchasing headaches and financial fiascos and we realized we had started businesses one week apart. Since then I have collaborated with her for various events with my company, introduced her to people who are now faithful and regular customers and share in her successes as she does mine. She provides a place for my events several times a year at no cost to me and often graciously prepares and donates a dish for my customers. Together we collaborate to bring out the best in both of our businesses and provide extra service for both of our customers.

Here are some effective ways to find someone and be someone who backs your business:

1. <u>Join a Group</u>   Often the small business world business is driven by referrals and connections. There are hundreds if not thousands of referral and networking groups across the globe geared toward small businesses.

Often the small business world business is driven by referrals and connections. There are hundreds if not thousands of referral and networking groups across the globe geared toward small businesses. They encourage a community of collaboration, support and most importantly referrals. Use the groups to build your relationships and gain advice from fellow entrepreneurs as well as help with issue like bookkeeping, website, social media marketing and more. There is a world of information walking around in these groups waiting to be shared. Much of it is free. To find these groups visit Meetup.com, your local chamber of commerce, your industry association, local coffee shop notice board or check online for a Small Business events calendar.

2. <u>Find an Online Community</u>
If your target market is outside the local community, or if you're uncomfortable with in-person events, try a social network or professional forum. There are many online communities and forums out there that encourage and support each other in developing their businesses, refer business to each other and build partnerships. Some examples include YoungEntrepreneur, and Entrepreneur magazine's Entrepreneur Connect. Also check out the many groups and forums across LinkedIn, Twitter and Facebook simply be utilizing the search bar.

3. <u>Give as Well as Receive</u>
When I say "be a backer" I mean give as well as receive. Like me with my lady at the Italian restaurant, networking is not a one-way relationship. It is as important to look for opportunities for fellow small businesses and make those connections as it is to receive them. As a bonus, by bringing opportunities to those in your network you attract attention to your business and bring it to the front of their minds.

4. Support Small Businesses

Support small business whenever possible. Adopt a 'support local, support small business' mindset as your business mantra. When conceivable seek to work with local independent businesses as your suppliers, vendors and service providers. Consider bartering. Bartering is a great way to collaborate, promote several businesses and help both businesses with overhead costs. If you are encouraging your clients to support (your) small businesses and work with you, it is important to listen to your own words and support other small businesses as well.

5. Create Your Own

Do you already have a set of local suppliers you trust, or a set of competitors who you would trust? Why not create your own network group and trade contacts and work with them? I have a friend who owns an event planning company. She has comprised a list of "preferred customers" that she offers her clients at no charge. This list includes small businesses that offer photography services, catering, entertainment, and DJ services and so forth. She gets no compensation for referring these businesses but should any of her clients utilize one of her preferred customers her business is represented as well as theirs. It's a win-win. Or it can be something as simple as writing for a magazine and promoting your business, guest blogging on other businesses blogs or what I do often is recommend the other businesses on Facebook and Twitter. If its national spaghetti, meatball, fettuccini day or anything like that I'm promoting my friend at the Italian restaurant. You can even partner with other small businesses where you only refer each other to clients providing each other with a small kick back for the referral.

Collaborating, connecting, and linking with other businesses brings added value to both you and your customers.

It also provides an opportunity for those businesses to expand the visibility of your business to their own clients and customers. So, find a tribe, build a tribe, be a backer. Support small business and let others support you as well.

RECAP: *No matter where you go, no matter what the weather, always bring your own sunshine.* (Anthony J. D'Angelo)

Chapter 5
Be transparent and vulnerable

Most people believe vulnerability is weakness. But really, vulnerability is courage. We must ask ourselves...are we willing to show up and be seen?
(Brene' Brown)

What comes to mind when you think of transparency? Webster defines it as: "fine or sheer enough to be seen through, free from pretense or deceit, easily detected or seen through, readily understood, characterized by visibility or accessibility of information especially concerning business practices."

Have you ever heard the phrase "there is trust in transparency?" As a small business owner, I have noticed that when I am transparent with people I encounter, when I let them know I do not have all the answers, that often I am "winging it" or "following my gut" they tend to find me more relatable. I think transparency frees any doubt of deceit or trickery where business relationships are concerned. Any business that wants to build and/or retain the trust of their customers should be working to improve transparency within their company.

Entrepreneurs are problem solvers. Often the problem they attempt to solve is one from personal experience. Being vulnerable and sharing your weaknesses and mistakes can be beneficial to the small business owner.

Opening our personal lives may not be for everybody nor necessarily good for every business, even in the over-sharing, social media world in which we live.

It's often a huge risk to bring our whole selves into our work, especially when hustling to make new connections. But consider this: By exposing your life, you may be helping others, especially those struggling with insecurities. Overcoming hesitations to "share it all" is good for most businesses because vulnerability often enhances the trust customers want and need in the founder or owner of the company and the products he/she sells.

I'd like to share insight from investor and entrepreneur Marcus Lemonis, CEO of Camping World, who says, *"So often in business we think that a very proper and stern way of conducting ourselves as know- it -all's and macho men and women is the way to be. But I believe that business is built on relationships. Relationships are built on trust, and trust is built on vulnerability."* He continues to say that talking to people about the rough patches in his life isn't so that people feel sorry for him but to create relatability between himself and people. *"The key to business isn't business. Rather, it's your understanding of people, how humans think, and more importantly how you think."* He often shares his story of being an orphan in Beirut and being adopted by an American family, sharing how fortunate he was to be in America but how different things were below the surface of how they seemed. He continued to say, *"We wake up every day and we try to be big leaders and put on a happy face for our employees and families because we don't want them to see weakness. I believe that that our weaknesses can be used as a sign of strength."* He often delegates others to share something with him that would make him want to do business with them.

Speaking to people coming out of college he informs them they cannot be an entrepreneur until they work for someone else. Being a business owner is about more than being a good boss or a bad boss. He tells them one of the hardest things about being a business owner is being a steward of other people.

 "If you're good to your customers (seems like something is missing in this quote – this is not a complete sentence when starting with If) you're good to your employees.

They matter more than the process or the product. Your success will not be defined by how much revenue you have but by your client roster and by the employees that you mentor who go on to open their own practices." Marcus urges other business owners to pay it forward to their clients. *"How do we get to more people quicker? Try to think about your small business owners differently than you used to."*

The days of "need to know" information is all but gone and a significant shift has recently occurred. In the age of technology where information is only a click away and social media platforms keep everyone connected 24/7 across the globe, we are entering a society that increasingly feels they need to know -- and share -- everything. But this expectation for transparency has extended beyond personal interactions and is becoming a reality in the business world. Transparency is proving important to a successful business model in all industries. This new era of consumers is techier, savvier, have more resources readily available than any other generation. Therefore, withholding or creatively reshaping information is no longer considered an option for them. As a business one quickly realizes that to build brand loyalty they first need to build trust.

A 2017 Entrepreneur article states that *"According to a recent study by Label Insight, up to 94 percent of consumers surveyed indicated that they were more likely to be loyal to a brand that offers transparency, while 73 percent said they were willing to pay more for a product that offers complete transparency."*

Article author, Larry Alton was quoted as saying, *"Transparency is important to consumers and employees alike. This open "reveal" of information shows that a company has nothing to hide, and helps consumers make better decisions -- so that, in a direct comparison, a company that reveals all information related to any specific area, will likely be chosen over a competitor that keeps its information secret."*

He went on to say that this concept of transparency has recently become a top priority since not even a decade ago, we personally felt the effects as we witnessed a global economic crash, due in part to greed, deceit or misleading financial institutions. We then depended on our trusted Wall Street investments, which belittled the wealth gap that we assumed we had created. It is not surprising that many Americans are under the assumption that corporations' goals are primarily focused only on profits. This focus, in turn makes the consumer (aka: customer) feel those goals could lead to unethical practices, especially if those practices are hidden from the public. In fact, often, customers are far more forgiving of mistakes if a company has a history of being forthright with all their interactions -- not just the negative ones. Through transparency, more companies will see success as they begin to view their customers as an extension of their internal operations teams.

So, instead of being fearful of transparency in your business, try to embrace it as way to improve service and increase customer loyalty. But transparency isn't just about customers. Employees highly value transparency in their interactions with management, going as far as determining its significant value in their happiness and satisfaction in the workplace. Employees want to work for a company when they know what it stands for and its long-term plans.

Regardless of the industry, here are a few simple steps any company of any size can take to become more transparent.

1. Be personally transparent
As a business owner, pick a (social media) platform or two and share your personal thoughts, ideas, likes, dislikes. The concept of transparency must start with you the business owner in an up close and personal way. And don't farm out your social media-- do it yourself! After all, it reflects YOU and no one knows you better. It's more personal coming directly from you not someone's perception of you, your company or brand.

2. Be internally transparent

Transparency starts from within YOU. If not everyone in your company believes you, the CEO, owner, president, etc., is transparent, then they will struggle portraying transparency to the marketplace (aka: your customers). Be an open book company and regularly update the entire staff on progress, risks and opportunities as well as have an open-door policy where employees know they can confidentially come to you with any matter business or personal.

3. Be transparent with your business objectives, goals and give updates

Let people know that you're trying to find a distributor or are short handed in the marketing department. Ask for help from your team, colleagues, and employees to take your quality to
another level. Most importantly, be careful to not make promises you may not be able to fulfill.

4 Be daring

As people come to trust you and your business through transparency, they will be more forgiving when you must explain why something didn't work or when a mistake occurred. Experiment with transparency and look for creative ways to develop a deeper, trust-building dialogue with your customers and staff.

As we can clearly see, transparency is a vital element in any business, not just as a marketing tactic. It is obvious that whether dealing with consumers or internal practices with employees, there is a need for businesses to meet the expectation of transparency in a real way.

I had a friend tell me once that she wanted to be a business that "stood for something." What is your backstory? Why do you do what you do? Are you making a difference in lives? Are you one of those entrepreneurs who shares their story as it relates to their vision or are you simply trying to be a millionaire before you're thirty?

Not that there is necessarily anything wrong with that but as you can see, sharing your background story can play an important role as part of your business operations, especially IF it is your why. For many, their story is the reason they started their business. As Marcus says, "Share your family story and your pluses and minuses."

RECAP: You belong somewhere you feel free, you belong among the wildflowers.

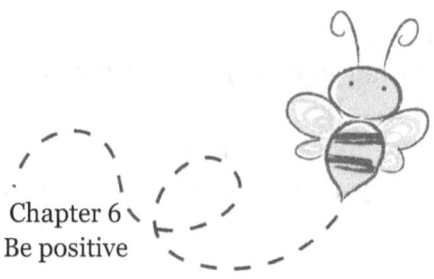

Chapter 6
Be positive

You cannot have a positive life and a negative mind.
(Joyce Meyer)

A positive mindset is critical in small business. Attitude makes all the difference. Things are going to happen, many not as you had planned or hoped. You cannot avoid those, but you can control how you react to them. When you're building a business, it would be great if everything worked perfectly, but let's be realistic, we know that's not the case. The journey is filled with difficult challenges, and sometimes they make us so frustrated that we want to give up.

Successful business owners, heck all successful people, don't focus on the negative, on what is not going right. Instead, they put their energy into moving their business forward, being a problem solver, finding a solution and coming up with a plan to conquer the demon.

When things go wrong, you have a choice: you can let it defeat you, or you can learn from the experiences and rise above. I love the quote by Henry Ford that says, "Whether you think you can, or you think you can't, you're right." Our attitude truly makes all the difference.
I have an Optimist Creed by Christian D. Larson that sits on my desk and I dissect it sentence by sentence every so often to keep my attitude of gratitude intact when I am feeling downtrodden or defeated.

It follows on the next page.

The Optimist Creed

Promise Yourself:
- To be so strong that nothing can disturb your peace of mind.
- To talk health, happiness, and prosperity to every person you meet.
- To make all your friends feel that there is something in them.
- To look at the sunny side of everything and make your optimism come true.
- To think only of the best, to work only for the best, and to expect only the best.
- To be just as enthusiastic about the success of others as you are about your own.
- To forget the mistakes of the past and press on to the greater achievements of the future.
- To wear a cheerful countenance at all times and give every living creature you meet a smile.
- To give so much time to the improvement of yourself that you have no time to criticize others.
- To be too large for worry, too noble for anger, too strong for fear and too happy to permit the presence of trouble.
- To think well of yourself and to proclaim this fact to the world, not in loud word, but in great deeds.
- To live in the faith that the whole world is on your side, so long as you are true to the best that is in you.

(The Optimist Creed was authored in 1912 by Christian D Larson in his book Your Forces and How to Use Them. It was adopted as Optimist International's creed in 1922. Many have found inspiration in the Optimist Creed. In hospitals, the creed has been used to help patients recover from illness. In locker rooms, coaches have used it to motivate their players.)

So, how's your attitude? Are you thinking positively about your business, its process, and its growth? Often, we are so right up against the glass we cannot see the good.

As a magazine publisher, not too long ago I was having a personal pity party with myself frustrated with the growth of my publication. It was during that time that I came across my very first issue.
I remembered how proud I was when I launched it and how much painstakingly effort was involved in its creation. But comparing that issue with the current issue encouraged me. The quality and growth were clearly visible, and my attitude changed. I went from frustrated because I thought I was not progressing fast enough to proud of my accomplishments in a matter of minutes.
I do not doubt that things have been and perhaps still are tough for us in small business. But we should rejoice that we are still standing! If you've been looking at your business as the glass half empty — focusing on the things you don't have or haven't accomplished — stop.

A pessimistic attitude reflects to your clients and employees. It hurts your sales, your company morale and productivity, and it is probably affecting your bottom line as well.
Of course, it's harder to remain optimistic when things are tough. Our most difficult moments often turn out to be blessings in disguise. Look for the silver linings. Besides, a positive attitude reduces stress.

The next time you find a negative mindset taking over your thought process and your business, try these:

1. <u>Choose to be positive.</u> Find a way to put a positive spin on whatever the situation. Look to see if there is a blessing hidden in there somewhere.

2. <u>Put it in perspective.</u> Even if you must tell yourself, "It could be worse." And uncover things that might actually make the situation worse.

3. <u>Act quickly.</u> Don't dwell on the situation. Learn from it, then quickly build your plan to move forward.

4. <u>Get rid of the toxic people.</u> If you've surrounded yourself with people who thrive on drama and trauma, remove them from your business before they suck the life out of you and your business.

5. <u>Celebrate your successes.</u> Remind yourself of the good things in your business (and your life). Even small accomplishments are steps toward bigger goals.

Difficult as it may be, try to keep a positive attitude whenever possible and you should find it has a huge impact on the overall success of your business. In keeping with the sunflower growing process and theme of this book, try to remember this: *"The tiny seed knew that to grow, it needed to be dropped in the dirt, covered with darkness, and struggle to reach the light."* (Sandra Kring)

RECAP: Everyday may not be a good day, but there is something good in every day. Find it. Reach for it.

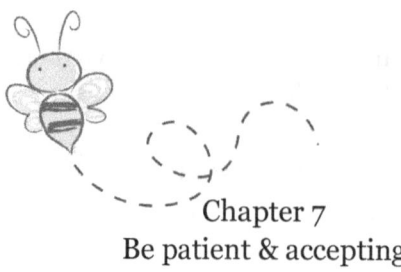

Chapter 7
Be patient & accepting

Be patient when it seems things are not going right and may never be right again. Accept that what is yours will come to you in the right way at just the right moment.
(Tyanla Vanzant)

I don't think I am alone when I say that as entrepreneurs, we are an impatient group. We want success now and fast. Entrepreneurs are used to pushing through and often expect our successes to reflect our efforts. But truly, the most important aspect of starting a business is patience.

As soon as you realize those good things are not going to happen overnight, that good things take time to grow, and that patience is the key to success the better you will be in your business dealings. We've all heard that patience is a virtue, which I wholeheartedly agree, but patience is also waiting… to continue when the going is hard and slow—that's patience. When you become an entrepreneur, most of your energy is focused on bringing in new business. We adopt a mentality that if we're not growing, we're dying plain and simple. We possess an attitude of "there is no time to wait." But soon we realize that to be successful, we must be patient, through the ups and downs. Sorry to break it to you but, you must accept that not every decision will go your way.

Look at impatience as self-sabotage. When you jump to a hasty decision, you create a false sense of time in your mind. When people or processes fail to meet that timeline, the mind can run wild.

You begin to question the motives and intentions of the people on the other side of the equation and put forth unreasonable expectations. This can lead to two unfortunate and unproductive outcomes.

First, it makes you look desperate. Pushing a partner too aggressively or issuing unreasonable ultimatums makes the situation looks precarious to others. These actions come across as a red flag and can quite often kill a sale.

Second, and most importantly, this kind of impatience is the ultimate self-sabotage. It clouds your judgement, detracts from your credibility, and damages your relationships. Remember, all good things take time and Rome wasn't built in a day. Nothing of value comes easily. In fact, anything of value requires time and effort, whether it's a matter of developing a skill, building a relationship, or launching a business.

Learning patience will serve you well—not just with gaining new business, but with building relationships. Most entrepreneurs get understandably frustrated and overwhelmed, given the financial burdens they face. Being patient will get you through those first couple of months or even years.

Patience really is a virtue. As entrepreneurs, we live in a world that values quick thinking and dynamic accomplishment. However, when you allow these traits to manifest in the form of impatience, that's typically when problems arise.

But think about this quote I heard, "How do you get the chicken? You need to hatch the egg, not smash it." Yes, starting a business is the most exciting thing you've probably ever done but patience will teach you how you need to change. Of course, there will always be some things simply just out of your control. You can't control everything.

So, step back and look at what you can control. When you are patient, you get better at taking the time to stop and focus on the now. And when you're in the now, you're mindful of the current circumstances. This helps you make wise, well-thought-out decisions.

RECAP: I'll end with a quote I love by Warren Buffett that says, *"No matter how great the talent or efforts, some things just take time. You can't produce a baby in one month by getting nine women pregnant."* Trust that though you may have a long road ahead, with continued hard work, dedication, and patience, you will get there... even if it takes baby steps. And remember, with perseverance even the snail made it to the ark.

For a quick pick-me-up on examining some successful businesses that failed and how they turned things around check out this site: https://www.gobankingrates.com/makingmoney/business/companies-failed-big-before-getting-right/

Chapter 8
Be brave

What lies behind us and what lies before us are small matters compared to what lies within us.
(Ralph Waldo Emerson)

As you have probably discovered, being an entrepreneur is not for the weary. One must grab their sword and shield daily and press through, especially on days when we don't feel like it. Of course, there will be boulders and obstacles that come our way. Everything from financing the vision to the wrong color printing on your brand's logo can send you into a tailspin at times. For many, being your own boss is a dream. It means the freedom and ability to call the shots, work your own hours, and (hopefully) be at the top of a profit-producing operation. But believe it or not, no matter how big or small your dream, your investment or your business, entrepreneurial triumph involves one thing: Risk.

What are you willing to risk? How much are you willing to sacrifice to make your dreams a reality? It truly comes down to risk. And by risk, I'm not talking about the irresponsible connotation of the term, but rather the mitigation of risk that coincides with personal sacrifices, with bravely going where you have never gone before and taken chances you probably have never taken.

If you need an example of such risk takers, consider Steve Jobs, a brilliant man that decided to skip college to pursue a risky tech venture, or Jeff Bezos who left his position as Vice President and moved miles away to build Amazon out of a garage or look at the creator of Dyson vacuums who was $4 million in debt after remortgaging his house to fund his prototypes. These examples are indications that when a stroke of genius collides with passion, as well as the willingness to risk everything and be brave, dreams become realities and success stories take place.

Another vital aspect of being bold, beyond taking risks and forcing yourself to get out of bed every morning, is ignoring the naysayers… that includes yourself (self- sabotage). I'd love to tell you that once you have this dream everyone will gather for TEAM YOU and will rally in support but in all honesty, more likely than not more people will tell you that you are off your rocker and crazy for taking such a leap and being so drastic. This often makes us question our purpose, our means and even our why. We start doubting our capabilities, talents and original vision. As I mentioned earlier, entrepreneurs are a rare and often misunderstood breed.

It can be hard to drown out the "naysayers" who ultimately can be deterring you from pursuing your passions. But if you make a conscious effort to stay positive and continue your relentless efforts, you will realize you're achieving the most important goal of all: staying true to you. It is imperative that you listen to yourself, have an advisory board, mentor or tribe to help lift you up when the weight gets heavy. Give yourself the advice you would give your friend. Trust your gut, shut out the naysayers, step out in faith, whatever that might mean to you, even if there is no clear path. You must lift that sword and be brave or you will never conquer the goal that lies ahead. The actions you take toward defeating every obstacle is more important than perfection, for every step no matter how small a step toward your end goal is one toward victory.

The publication Inc.com approached a few fellow entrepreneurs, and this is their advice for ignoring negative feedback as you pursue the plight of entrepreneurship:

1. <u>Free yourself from others' opinions.</u> *"It wasn't until I freed myself of caring about what others without buy-in thought of me or my work that I was able to really push forward with my companies. If you're always looking backward and paying attention to the negative chatter of people who are more interested in spending their energy cutting you down than doing something for themselves, you'll be carrying around a huge ankle weight."*

2. <u>Focus on the worst-case scenario.</u> *"It may sound negative, but I find worst-case thinking is useful for combatting fears. For most people, the worst-case scenario of their business failing is going back to a job like the one they're currently in! Most people have irrational fears like being abandoned by friends and family or never being able to start another business. It's useful to sit down and realize that these fears aren't true."*

3. <u>It only takes one "yes" to change your life.</u> *"It doesn't matter how many people tell you "no," because it only takes one "yes" to change your life forever. Dozens of people told me launching ZinePak was a terrible idea, but I kept going until I got the only "yes" that mattered, from a music buyer at Walmart. That "yes" meant more than 1,000 "no's because it was actionable. Find the actionable "yes" for your dream and ignore the other noise."*

4. <u>Talk to other entrepreneurs.</u> *"The general population is much more likely to be full of naysayers than people who have actually built businesses. Surround yourself with other business owners -- but if they all think your idea doesn't have legs, you should probably listen to them."*

5. <u>If you have a cash runway, you can afford to take risks.</u> *"The naysayers are most likely worried about the financial burden of starting a company. You can dream big and still be pragmatic about starting your business so that you're not throwing yourself into a mountain of debt and despair if it doesn't work out. Save up six months' worth of living expenses so you can stay calm and confident while you focus on growing your new business."*

6. <u>Defiance is an integral part of a founder's DNA.</u> *"In my 20 years' experience as a five-time founder, I've learned that successful founders are innately motivated and even driven by naysaying and rejection, whereas poor founders have a regressive reaction to negativity, and oftentimes too easily surrender to pushback. Great founders want to win all the time, and even more so when they're told that they can't win or shouldn't try."*

7. <u>Remember that the 'brick walls' are there for a reason.</u> *"Naysayers are awesome -- they're a free focus group. You just have to remember (quoting Randy Pausch here) that the brick walls are there for a reason. They let us know how bad we want something. Naysayers are identifying the problems with your idea. Your job as an entrepreneur is to recognize that problems are just opportunities in disguise. Naysayers build the walls; entrepreneurs scale them."*

8. <u>Stay positive.</u> *"The naysayers only give you the reasons why your business won't work, but you need to focus on what will work about it and how to make that happen. Staying proactive and positive in your thinking can motivate you to pursue that dream and prove to others that they were wrong about their reasons why not to do it."*

9. <u>Remember your passion</u>. *"The whole world will be eager to tell you how your idea will fail. Remember why you're passionate about the company you're building. The day I realized I could make a difference to others was the day the company became much bigger than me. I had to push on. Eventually, I met the right people to help me move the company forward."*

RECAP: You will never be brave if you don't take chances and risk getting hurt. You will never learn if you don't make mistakes and you will never be successful if you don't encounter and even embrace failure.

Chapter 9
Be willing to fail

*I've missed more than 9,000 shots in my career.
I've lost almost 300 games. 26 times, I've been trusted to
take the game winning shot and missed.
I've failed, over and over again.
That is why I succeed.*
(Michael Jordan)

Yes, you read that correctly. And we just mentioned about being brave and winning in the previous chapter so why discuss failure as an option? Because we must be realistic. We ARE going to make mistakes. We WILL fail. But rest assured, it's not the end of your business if that happens. In fact, it's okay to accept failure when you're a small business. Failures allow you a chance to examine what NOT to do, what went wrong, what worked and what you should do. Studies show that companies that observe their failures are far more likely to succeed than those that don't. With over half of small businesses failing within the first five years this almost seems like a no-brainer. The importance is knowing how to fail well rather than overlooking the risks in the first place.

One of the benefits of business incubators is that they provide an opportunity for reflection on failure, in an environment that, while supportive, will challenge ideas. We've heard plenty of stories of people who've failed once and come back all the stronger for it.

The first thing most entrepreneurs fail to do when starting a business is research. Just because you love making flower arrangements does not mean you should open a florist. Try working Mother's Day or Valentine's day at a local florist and see how much you enjoy it at the end of the day.

Research your competition. Discover what sets the areas florists apart from each other and see if there is something different that you can offer that the area is not yet receiving. It is vital to get advice from others in your industry and discuss their difficulties, struggles, and triumphs. Have others in your trade examine your idea to help you notice problems with a concept early on before you take on the costs associated with a launch. Consider seeking funding and investment advice before you spend resources you may not have. It's also essential to build your awareness of the competition, and others who may move into the same space. Just because your concept was unique when it was first conceived, does not mean it will be that way a few months down the road. It can be heart-wrenching abandoning a project after putting so much into it, but sometimes the best decision is knowing when not to proceed.

Secondly, even with all the research in the world, you may have to come to grips with the fact that your big idea won't catch on. There's no shame in failure for this reason. In fact, that failure could possibly keep you from making a plethora of other, more detrimental ones.

Utilize failures to seek new opportunities. I'm a firm believer that if a door isn't opening it's not your door. But often we get so caught up in the closed door we lose sight of the one opening right in front of us. Seek out collaborations or other entrepreneurs that you may be able to partner with utilizing your talents.
By failing to accept that you must do it all on your own, you could be denying yourself a great opportunity at the expense of pride. Besides, failing is much easier and more productive when accomplished as a team effort. Running a business is much easier when you aren't doing it all on your own.

Working with partners whom you trust and whose skills complement yours is a good way to mitigate against failure. On your own, it's easy to dwell on what you think you did wrong or avoid thinking about your mistakes.

With a partner or partners, you simply acknowledge the failure and move on. Discussing things honestly and directly with partners helps you analyze your successes and mistakes, decide what will be different next time and the changes needed to get there.

You must not hide your past failures.

It is all a question of positioning. Experience and failure are different sides of the same coin. In either context, past failures can prove valuable. For example, you can share with others what you have learned on your journey, rather than why you have failed. By turning a negative into a positive in this way, entrepreneurs can demonstrate credibility as a more seasoned business professional. All entrepreneurs need to learn to not be so scared of failure. Any experienced business person understands that you cannot guarantee success. You can make all the right decisions, manage your business perfectly and still fail. By embracing this fact, entrepreneurs can turn adversity into advantage and obstacles into opportunities. A good entrepreneur will understand what went wrong, learn from the experience, and avoid failing for the same reason twice. After all, good judgment comes from experience. Experience comes from bad judgment.

So, don't be afraid of failure. In short, don't fail to prepare and plan but be aware of how many times you've failed at the same thing. Most of all, remember that how you react to failure, and how it shapes what you do next, are the real indicators of your business success.

RECAP: Failure defeats losers but inspires winners.

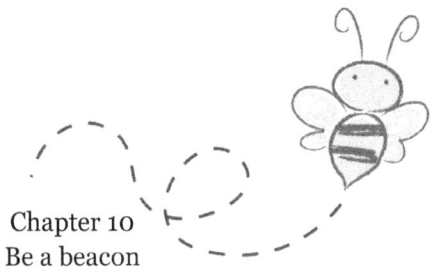

Chapter 10
Be a beacon

You are the salt of the earth and the light of the world.
(Matthew 5:13-16)

Truly, the goal for any successful professional is to become a shining light in their field or industry. These are individuals with followings and a voice that is infectious and charismatic, that resonates beyond their borders. They unapologetically lead and set the direction for others.

Establishing yourself as a beacon does miracles for your reputation and credibility, which directly translates to business success. But while there is no proven path to becoming such a light, connecting with and engaging others similarly yoked is an important part of building a name for yourself.

A popular method of producing such results involves quoting your industry favorites in articles, broadcasts, and publications. Professional leaders love being quoted as this strengthens their status, and many will be glad to share words of wisdom with your audience. These leaders, in turn, might share your piece with their followers, and may link to your content or publicly endorse it. As the result, some of their "charm" may rub off on you and your business.

Business beacons also add value to conversations in your industry. The point is, that by being a beacon, you're taking the knowledge and experiences you've gained in the industry and sharing them with others for educating and engaging, not selling or self-promotion.

Being a beacon or light is all about giving without asking for anything in return. Helping others get to their goals is immensely satisfying. Be the example. People will often follow those whose values, choices and actions align with theirs.

Beacon entrepreneurs provide value personally and professionally to others through quality content. If you focus on producing high-value and actionable content that your audience can pick up and implement within their business, something that can make a difference in the immediate future, then you're sharing a luminated light that is not easily duplicated but is highly coveted and intensely respected and revered. Anyone can sell a product or share an experience, but what separates the beacons from the wannabes is the deep insight and experience of the subject at hand that they share with those they encounter.

Consider being a mentor, making a difference to get your light shining. The true entrepreneur not only invests in their own development, but they also help others grow. As the saying goes, "when one teaches, two learn."

Remember, it takes time, invested time. Volunteer. Mentor. Teach. Successful business leaders tend to agree that what is most important is to focus more on giving, rather than receiving. Working every day toward shining that light and making that impact can be a long journey. It starts with daily personal development, writing and publishing content, helping and mentoring others, continuously improving yourself, networking tirelessly and working your way up to respect and trust. It is a lot of hard work, but it is equally rewarding for the select few who become business beacons. For the trail they leave behind is bright.

In closing, as you embrace this journey I first want to congratulate you on taking the initial step by purchasing this little book. By doing so you have indicated that you want to be a better person and a business that leaves legacies.

As you have probably discovered, you are in for a roller coaster ride like you have never experienced. Filled with ups and downs, twists and turns leaving you both nauseated and thrilled at the same time. It is an unexplainable adventure for anyone who has never purchased a ticket for the ride. I hope this book will serve as not only a guide to you in answering some preliminary questions but also a resource for you to refer and glean information from time to time, that the pages will be underlined, dog-eared and notes made in the margins of things you want to remember and will access often.

Most of all, I want to leave you with this short little list:

10 extra tidbits of advice:

1. <u>Start every day as a new day.</u> By starting your day with the odometer at zero allows you to generate a sense of accomplishment and moving forward.

2. <u>Ask for help.</u> It's all right to admit you do not know everything. I know it's your baby but if you're busy dealing with things you are ill-equipped for then the business suffers. Find someone you trust and delegate.

3. <u>Pause.</u> Breathe and ask questions. Get help with decision-making and operational goals.

4. <u>Stay tenacious.</u> Stay true to your idea. Rinse. Reexamine. Repeat.

5. <u>Be selective but not exclusive</u>. Accept the clients you wish to attract and the employees you desire but not to the point that you are so unreachable you dismiss or overlook talent and potential.

6. <u>Choose a team that challenges you</u>. You want to surround yourself with people who will push and challenge you. Choose mentors, investors, coaches, and advisors, who have broad vantage points and long histories of watching companies rise and fall. You want people in your circle who have seen enough to know they've seen too much, and who will talk you into pushing yourself as a result.

7. <u>Stay focused.</u> The focus is about aligning with your purpose. When actions reflect intentions, you will be in alignment with your personal mission. It is then that you can truly shine.

8. <u>Get out and stay out.</u> Visit your competitors, network with other entrepreneurs, shake hands with potential clients and customers. If you promise people something, deliver it. Plain and simple. Be the FACE of your brand.

9. <u>Ask open-ended questions.</u> To your staff, your customers and yourself. Avoid yes or no questions. Your goal should be to enable and normalize very human feelings and let them direct the conversation for a bit.

10. <u>Stay consistent in your brand</u>. When it comes to building a brand, that feels like a credible, legitimate company is behind it, one that people feel like they can trust — consistency is everything.

Above all else, every day in every situation ask yourself these three questions:

1. <u>What signal am I emitting?</u> (Emotional) how are you feeling regarding your business? Confused or clear-minded? Anxious or excited? Angry or empowered? Sad or joyful? Make sure you are releasing good and/or powerful emotions in every aspect of your brand from your smile to your social media.

2. <u>Which reality am I congregating with?</u> (Imaginative) Are you imagining your business thriving and successful or repeatedly struggling? Do you see yourself making money in your business or barely getting by? If you wish to have more money try not to focus so much on the lack of it. See yourself as that which you wish to be or engage with.

3. <u>Am I in my finite or infinite mind?</u> (Thought) Are your thoughts limited and restricted? i.e. how, who, what, when. Or are they worrisome and fearful? Are they unlimited, trusting, full of faith and confidence? DO you vision yourself in the world of possibilities where anything can happen at any time and anyplace or can you not see beyond your circumstances today?

RECAP: There are two ways of spreading light, to be the candle or the mirror that reflects it. Which are you?

As you embark on whatever journey you're taking, whatever seed you are planting, watering, or nurturing, I want to say congratulations!! Congratulations on the first step. I was well into my fifties before I really came into my purpose as a person and an entrepreneur and quickly realized I was born to be in business for myself.

It is my hope that you found some nuggets in this little book that will take root as you press forward in your journey. As well, it is my heart's desire that you "Be" successful in your new endeavor but most of all, may you "Be" happy in your soul.

Other books by this author:

God, Are You Listening?

Rambling Roads

In An Instant

Walking In My Mind

Raised by Gypsies, Surrounded by Dreamers, Rooted a Rebel

Her published works can be found at:
Amazon.com/author/cmichellebryant
Or check out her blog, Girl, it's time to focus on the sparkle
www.facebook.com/Girlitstimetofocusonthesparkle/

Additional entrepreneurial resources- available online:

- Forbes.com
- Entrepreneur.com
- Small businessbc.com
- Smallbusiness.chron.com
- Cnbc.com
- Infoentrepreneurs.org/
- Moz.com
- Fastcompany.com
- Realbusiness.com
- Blogs.constantcontact.com
- Melissaforziatevents.com
- Smallbusiness.com
- Inc.com/young-entrepreneur

www.ingramcontent.com/pod-product-compliance
Lightning Source LLC
Chambersburg PA
CBHW070941220526
45469CB00007B/2473